Stuart McAlpine

Asking

for Pastors

*"He will stand and shepherd His flock
in the strength of the Lord...
and they will live securely."*
(Micah 5:4)

www.asknetwork.net

© 2016 Stuart McAlpine

All rights reserved. No part of this publication may be reproduced, stored in a retrieval system, or transmitted in any form or by any means, electronic, mechanical, photocopying or otherwise, without the prior written consent of Ask Network.

All scripture quotations are from the Holy Bible, New International Version, Copyright © 1973, 1978, 1984, 2011 by Biblica, Inc.™ Used by permission.

ISBN 978-1-4951-9883-0

Quotations from *Working the Angles* by Eugene Petersen (Eerdmans Publishing Company)
Biblical Eldership by Alexander Strauch (Lewis and Roth Publishers); *Prayer for Pastors* (A sermon by James Smith 1858)

Cover design and layout by Pete Berg

TABLE OF CONTENTS

1. The Heating Plant 5

2. Immigration and Customs 11

3. What Do You Mean By Pastor? 15

4. Asking That Pastors Be (Part 1) 19

5. Asking That Pastors Be (Part 2) 27

6. Ask God That Pastors Do (Part 1) 29

7. Ask God That Pastors Do (Part 2) 35

8. Why Do Sheep Scatter? 39

9. The Appeal: Ask For Pastors ... Ask For Us 47

10. The Altar Call: Who Will Ask? 51

11. Closing Prayers 55

    Appendix 59

1 THE HEATING PLANT

> *"The biblical fact is that there are no successful churches. There are, instead, communities of sinners, gathered before God week after week in towns and villages all over the world. The Holy Spirit gathers them and does His work in them. In these communities of sinners, one of the sinners is called pastor and given a designated responsibility ... to keep the community attentive to God."*
> — Eugene Petersen

Sometimes we need to begin by stating the obvious. Pastors are sinners saved by grace, like all other believers. Pastors are Christians before they are characterized by any other designation. There can be no calling if there is no conversion. If there is no conviction in the heart of the pastor there can be no confirmation of his ministry by the congregation. Over 1500 years ago, St. Augustine preached a sermon about pastors based on that most important chapter on 'shepherding', Ezekiel 34, and he addressed the congregation as follows: *"We are Christians for our own sake. We are leaders for your sake. The fact that we are Christians should serve our own advantage. The fact that we are leaders should serve only yours."*

When this simple truth is forgotten, more attention is paid to a pastor's position in the church than his position in Christ.

The duties of the ministry begin to outrun the devotion of the heart, and commitment to ministry goals displaces communion with God. How easily a work for God can become a substitute for a walk with God. How unintentionally does the flock's need for the pastor's attention displace the Father's need for the pastor to be attentive to Him. How imperceptibly does the organic and corporate body of Christ become an organized corporation. How unconsciously are ministering pastors expected to become mediating priests. How subtly does the call to lead the flock, become the temptation to lord it over them. How neglectfully does the joy of worship become the duty of work. How insidiously does hidden sin become public shame. How gradually does the flame of all-in pastoring become the ashen face of a burnt-out pastor. Will you pray for pastors?

How would you write a pastor's job-description? What are you asking of pastors? What does that tell you about what you need to be asking of God for them? You may be clearer about what you are asking of the pastor, than what you are asking of God for the pastor? Spurgeon rehearsed some of the expectations of pastors to his ministerial students: *"To face the enemies of truth, to defend the bulwarks of the faith, to rule well in the house of God, to comfort all that mourn, to edify the saints, to guide the perplexed, to bear with the forward, to win and nurse souls — all these and a thousand other works beside are not for a Feeble-mind or a Ready-to-halt, but are reserved for a Great-heart whom the Lord has made strong for himself. Seek then strength from the Strong One."* There is no seeking for strength for the pastor without asking for it. Listen to Jesus praying for Pastor Peter: *"I have prayed for you that your faith may not fail, and when you have turned back, strengthen your brothers."* (Luke 22:32) Without that asking for strength, there is no pastoral strengthening of others. With pastors as our focus, we need to ask like Paul: *"I pray that out of His glorious riches He may strengthen you with power through His Spirit in your inner being."* (Ephesians 3:16) When his fear was that he would get too weak to complete the work, Nehemiah *"prayed, 'Now strengthen my hands.'"* (Nehemiah

6:9) The strengthening of the pastorate is the answer to the asking of *"the Strong One"* on their behalf.

When we intercede for the church, we must pray biblically and specifically for those who are entrusted by God to care for the sheep of His pasture. When we pray for someone to become a Christian, we should pray for the pastors who will nurture them and enfold them in the love of Jesus. Tragic events in the lives of many ministers and ministries serve to persuade us that we must plead for those who lead. Many are the never-ending demands of pastoral ministry. I remember my father describing Moses waking up in the morning and lifting his tent-flap and saying, "Oh no! They're still there!" Of course, with pressures there are always privileges, but pastoral pressures do not cease, therefore nor should our prayers for them.

You might think it is obvious to pray for pastors, given their very public role in the community, but the premise of this appeal is that pastors are most often the least prayed for member of a church community. For most of them there would be little comfort in a show of hands of those who prayed for them on a daily basis, or any basis at all for that matter. Of course, asking for pastors needs to begin with the humbling of a pastor that asks for prayer himself — a pastor like me. I wrote this booklet when I was in the first year of a church-plant in Washington DC in the year 1988, and that was way long enough to convince me of my desperate need for covering and empowering prayer. Who was asking for me? How was I asking for myself? What you are about to read came out of some of my meditations and was meant as a kick-start for my congregants to ask for me as well as for other pastors. Somehow it has run through two prints of 10,000 copies each, which would seem to suggest a deep need. After nearly thirty years of pastoral ministry, this has been reprinted with few substantive changes or additions. I can still attest to the need for everything that it suggests should be asked for, and I am an even needier candidate for it now than then.

Writing in 1858, James Smith had a passion to get people to pray for pastors. As a pastor himself, he knew what he was talking about and he did not mince words: *"Allow me to ask, How much do you pray for your minister? He fills an arduous post. His is a glorious but a solemn, and difficult work. He has to watch for souls, as one who must give account. He has taken the oversight, and is expected to be an example to the flock. On him, in a very important sense, your comfort, edification, and growth in grace depends. He needs great grace, special assistance, and indomitable courage. He has, in a peculiar sense, to do battle with the principalities and powers in the Heavenly places. He has to bear with much from every member of the Church, and more from the whole flock. He is often bowed down under a sense of his unfitness for the work, and oppressed with a sense of its overwhelming importance. He is often among his people, as Paul was: in weakness, and fear, and much trembling. He sees more imperfections in his poor sermons than his people see, and finds more faults with his ministrations in private, than they do in public. With what bitterness of soul he often asks, "Who has believed our report, and to whom is the arm of the Lord revealed?" He dreads the thought of his gifts decaying, his graces withering, or his usefulness decreasing. He travails in birth for many, he stands in doubt of many, while he longs for the salvation of all. O how solemn it often appears to him, to stand between the living God, and sinners dead in trespasses and sins; to be put in trust with the gospel, charged to be faithful unto death; and to realize, as at times he does, that that gospel will either be a savor of life unto life, or of death unto death. Brethren, beloved of the Lord, with such views of your pastors' position and feelings before you, I again affectionately ask, How much do you pray for your pastors? Do you pray for them as their office and work demand? Do you pray for them as they entreat and beseech you to do? Do you pray for them now, as you once did? Do you pray for them as your conscience will admit you should? Do you pray for them, as perhaps, on your own death-bed, or when God is about to take them away from you — you will wish you had? Would not many of your past hours have been better spent in prayer for your pastors, than in talking about them as you did? Have you not wasted many an hour, which might have been spent with much profit to yourself, and benefit to them — if spent in praying for your pastor."* I have read his complete message and I can tell you he is just warming up here. So the question is: do you pray for pastors?

I know you have heard of Spurgeon but probably have no clue about this James Smith, who happened to precede "the prince of preachers" at the Metropolitan Tabernacle in London by four years. The extraordinary harvest of Spurgeon's ministry was unequaled in England. But here's the thing. When asked once about the spiritual success of his ministry, Spurgeon took the enquirers down into the church basement to what he called his spiritual "heating plant." It was where the furnace was situated and it has been estimated that there would be as many as four hundred people in there, praying for him and for the message he would soon be delivering. Is it any wonder that there was not a chair in that huge church where someone had not committed their life to Christ? Is it any surprise that Spurgeon's preaching and teaching legacy remains a spiritual inheritance for every new generation of pastors. I have a hunch that it was the unknown James Smith, with his passion for pastors to be prayed for, expressed in his sermons and pamphlets that asked people to ask for pastors, that laid the foundation in that community of faith for what was to come, that would impact a nation and generations.

Later in his ministry, on an occasion when Spurgeon was lecturing to a new generation of trainee pastors and passing on his pastoral wisdom, he recounted the following story that he had read only the day before: *"A certain preacher, whose sermons converted men by scores, received a revelation from heaven that not one of the conversions was owing to his talents or eloquence, but all to the prayers of an illiterate lay-brother, who sat on the pulpit steps, pleading all the time for the success of the sermon. It may in the all-revealing day be so with us. We may discover, after having labored long and wearily in preaching, that all the honor belongs to another builder, whose prayers were gold, silver, and precious stones, while our sermonizing, being apart from prayer, were but hay and stubble."* Again, he knew the need of pastors to be prayed for.

The following notes are offered as a small fire-starter for your pastor's "heating plant." The intent is that you will be encouraged to pray the scriptures and develop a Holy Spirit directed prayer strategy for your pastor and all pastors. Your own study and meditation in the Word, your personal experience of the church and her ministry, your love for your pastor/s will serve to amplify the scant headlines that follow, and thus extend the range of your intercession for both pastor and pasture.

If you are a pastor reading this, then there is no harm in being encouraged to ask for yourself, before you ask others to ask for you. As John Owen put it: *"No man preacheth his sermon well to others if he doth not first preach it to his own heart."*

2 Immigration and Customs

Before we go a step further, I think it would be good to stop and check up on two things: our citizenship and our baggage.

Our citizenship

It has been said that we live in a time when many have said 'yes' to Jesus but 'no' to the church. My concern at this check-point is not to catalogue the reasons for this, be they understandable, forgivable or patently unacceptable. The gospel does not recognize a privatized salvation that can function outside a spiritual family. The reconciliation effected by the cross has two planes: vertical (communion with God restored) and horizontal (community with others restored.) It is therefore impossible to have a high view of Christ and a low view of His church. To be in Christ is to be in the family of God. The Christian community of faith puts on display the purpose of God *"to create in Himself one new man."* (Ephesians 2:15) Paul goes on to use three images or models to describe our participation in this new creation, and the privileges that go with it. We are:

- citizens of a kingdom — this speaks of our security;
- family members of a household — this speaks of our intimacy;
- bricks in a building — this speaks of our community.

Are you enjoying the delights and experiencing the

demands of your membership in the body of Christ? Are you committed whole-heartedly to a local expression of God's incredible family where you know you have been placed for this season of your life? I'm not asking you about your view of church government, whether it be Episcopalian, Congregational, Presbyterian, Independent, Church Planting Movement, Apostolic or Chaotic. I'm not asking if your preference is expositional, experiential, existential, experimental, expansional, exponential or just expendable. Are you in amazed awe of God's purposes in and through the church? What are your convictions about the church and your attitudes towards it? Are you incorporated or isolated? It will affect how you pray for pastors.

Our baggage

Are you carrying any baggage as far as your attitude is concerned toward either the church or church leadership in general, or toward a particular pastor? Have you ever had a heart-hardening experience, or at least been tempted to, because of your reaction, justified or not, to certain pastoral leaders? In my pastoral experience I have noted distinctive stages in the process of dislodgement from church involvement, that someone goes through when unresolved offence discolors, distorts and ultimately destroys the offended person's view of church community. This is not limited by any means to historic denominations, but has been arguably as common in new church planting movements and national ministry movements during the last thirty years. Those who should be citizens begin to live like aliens, when they sin, or are sinned against in the church. People become:

- *Disappointed* — Joyful hopes, enthusiastic commitment and legitimate expectations (whether for relationship, discipleship or whatever) begin to be bruised or eroded as unfulfillment and unanswered concerns start to bring frustration and disappointment.

- *Disillusioned* — Fundamental beliefs and convictions about what church life and leadership should and could look like are shaken, and this can open the door to cynicism and disillusion.

- *Disaffected* — Whatever affects our beliefs then affects our sense of belonging and there is often a consequent sense of estrangement in relationships with leaders and fellow congregants.

- *Disabled* — Withdrawal from fellowship dislocates people from their involvement and spiritual productivity in the body of Christ, immobilizing their giftedness and causing spiritual ineffectiveness.

- *Dimembered* — The awful possibility is that someone may cut themselves off from fellowship altogether, and cease to assemble with the saints, resulting sometimes in a grievous tearing from the body, whether the separation is sudden or a slow demise. Relational separation of any kind never happens along clean-cut lines.

I have encountered many unresolved reactions to the above experiences: distrust of church leadership, defensiveness of personal spirituality, disinterest in church involvement, dislike for church members who do not see it their way, disloyalty to the church, disassociation from it and instead, association with any number of groups or causes that satisfy personal spiritual interests and needs only. I have wept with backsliders who have confessed their anger and unrepentant bitterness towards a church, as well as with full-time church workers who have suffered the wounds of rejection. The majority of such attitudes are directed toward church leadership, and in most cases toward particular pastors. Similarly, there are pastors who have been disenchanted in their own view of God's family, either because of their own sin, or because of the way that they have been treated by congregations.

Before we pray for pastors it is important to check our baggage.

Sadly, legitimate authority can be illegitimately exercised. There are two equal and opposite dangers. Leaders can abuse authority, dominate people and fail to serve. People can deny leadership, refuse authority and fail to support. Someone has wisely said that it is as wrong to impose leadership simply because it is God-given, as it is to oppose it because it happens to be imperfect. It is the responsibility of both pastors and people to confess sin committed against God and against each other, to forgive both offender and offense, and to reconcile with each other. There is healing for oppressed people and oppressive leaders.

If we are assured about our citizenship and have passed the spiritual customs inspection of our baggage, then we will have freedom in asking for pastors.

3 What Do You Mean By Pastor?

"Paul sent to Ephesus for the elders ... the Holy Spirit has made you overseers. Be shepherds of the church of God, which he bought with His own blood."
— Acts 20: 17. 28

By nature, although we love titles and honorable designations, Jesus' warning against being called 'rabbi' makes a lot of sense. (Matthew 23:8) Those who are ordained to the ministry suddenly become 'Rev' which neither means that they are to be 'revered' or assumed to be 'revived'! Arthur Pink wrote: *"In ourselves we are poor, sinful erring creatures, and daily do we have occasion to blush and hang our heads in shame. Therefore we respectfully request that none will address us as 'Reverend'. No worm of the dust is due such a title."* You could trust Spurgeon to have a thought: *"I very much demur to the designation, 'To the Reverend C. H. Spurgeon,' for no 'reverence' is due to me! Assuredly, 'Reverend' and 'sinner' make a curious combination. And as I know I am the second, I repudiate the first ... 'holy and REVEREND is His name.' Psalm 111:9."* There may be some who derive a sense of security from titles and need the description to somehow establish who they are in relationship to others. There are some who bear titles that fit neither the person nor the ministry. There is always a danger that 'pastor' that legitimately describes a function, becomes 'Pastor' which designates a hierarchical position. Very soon the new covenant 'pastor' becomes a synonym for the old covenant 'priest'. However, there is a pragmatic convenience in a nomenclature that helps to identify who's who and that truthfully describes a person's calling. The problem arises when a term that is useful for identification purposes becomes a necessity for establishing a pastor's sense of identity. My point is that though such designations may be organizationally functional, they are not scripturally necessary.

'Pastor' in this booklet is not limited to those who bear the title because they have theologically graduated and been suitably certificated and denominationally inducted. As important and legitimate as such training and consecration may be, they do not of themselves constitute either a call or an equipping for pastoral ministry. We should acknowledge the specific ministry of *"pastor"* (Ephesians 4:1) and remember that it is a gift of the risen Christ to the church. However, we must also acknowledge the interchangeable (though not synonymous) terms of *"overseer… elder…shepherd"* (Greek: *episkopos, presbuteros, poimen*) which, though distinctive terms, combine in their meanings to give a complete picture of the pastoral leader's oversight, position and function. I am not suggesting that there is an equality of pastoral ability in all elders. There may well be a diversity of giftedness. In this presentation our expectation is that there will be a plurality of elders in a local congregation, the context for safety, effectiveness, maturity and accountability of all pastoral leadership. All those who exercise pastoral ministry in the local church are the concern of this booklet, be they full-time 'pastors', who are clearly more visible in public ministry, or less public 'elders' who support themselves through full-time or part-time employment, but who nonetheless labor among the flock, and share an equality of ministry status, if not an equality of responsibility, with the full-time pastors. In the church I serve, a pastor is first set apart as an elder. A practice that has always served me well is to have my name simply included alphabetically in the list of elders, with an asterisk that indicates which elders are full-time. If they are all called, scripturally qualified and ministering, then they are all equally worthy of our prayers, that they all be pastors who take heed of themselves, who feed the sheep and lead the flock.

4 Asking That Pastors Be (Part 1)

So who should pastors aspire to be like? There are many temptations and expectations to model oneself after well-known charismatic figures, leaders of spiritual movements, spokespersons for particular doctrinal emphases, advocates of church-growth philosophies, the voices and faces of Christian media. As encouraging, edifying and educative as these examples may be, to emulate them is to set the sights too low.

Models are one thing; molds are another. There are many influences in the church and in the world that seek to shape pastors into their own image by insisting that they pour their lives into forms that suit the desires of men or movements, rather than satisfy the demands of God; that may sentence them to human subservience rather than free them for divine service; that may expect them to follow the strictures formulated by men, more than the scriptures inspired by the Holy Spirit. Essentially, we must pray that pastors be like Jesus and manifest the shepherding characteristics of His ministry. Robert Murray McCheyne, an asking pastor if ever there was one, wrote: *"It is not great talents God blesses so much as a likeness to Jesus. A holy minister is an awful weapon in the hand of God."*

In the New Testament there are four important descriptions of Jesus as shepherd, and in every case, the immediate context has to do with the necessity of the sacrifice of His life at the cross. The crook of the shepherd cannot be separated from the cross of

Christ. Talking of sacrifice, Pastor Willie Still of Aberdeen (under whose preaching my father gave his life to Christ), reminded his readers in his book *The Work of a Pastor*: *"Israel's sheep were reared, fed, tended, retrieved, healed and restored for sacrifice on the altar of God."* The sacrifice of the Shepherd for the sheep would make possible the sacrificial offering of themselves to God. As we look at these references and use them as an asking guide, let us affirm at the outset that if the cross of Christ is applied to the pastor's life and preached from the pulpit, then there is a holy standard for both sheep and shepherd. There is plenty to preach about, but as Don Carson has noted so powerfully in his book *The Cross and Christian Ministry*, we live in a culture in which talk about issues displaces the teaching of the gospel. A new crisis deflects attention from the old cross. Ask for a recovery of the preaching of Christ crucified and risen, for this will guard the heart of the pastor who speaks it, and the hearts of the sheep in the pasture who hear it. The words of Jennie Evelyn Hussey's hymn are to the point:

> *"Lest I forget Gethsemane*
> *Lest I forget thy agony*
> *Lest I forget thy love for me*
> *Lead me to Calvary."*

We are going to use these four passages to help us to ask God for pastors. My suggested 'ask-points' are not exhaustive, so I invite you to go to each passage, read it and meditate on it, and then pray the Word specifically for the pastor/s on your mind.

Jesus is the GOOD SHEPHERD: He will redeem
"I am the good shepherd. The good shepherd lays down His life for the sheep." (John 10:11)

Clearly, pastors cannot redeem anyone but they can declare Jesus' redemption through their communication of lip and life. They should never forget the price that was paid in order for them to minister. Truly it is *"through God's mercy we have this* ministry." (2 Corinthians 4:1) There is ground for neither arrogance nor independence. The mark of the cross in his life was for Paul the ultimate proof of his calling. The redeeming and cleansing power of that cross must be the pastor's present experience. As St. Gregory put it: *"The hand that means to make another clean must not itself be dirty."* I once read a poignant story about a western pastor who went to an African nation to preach. He presented his best and most effective messages with verve and volubility, but at the end of the meeting, an old African saint looked up at him and said, *"I heard what you said, Sir, and it was fine, but I did not see the wounded hands."* Read and meditate on Jesus' message about the shepherd and his flock in John 10: 1-18.

Ask God for pastors:

- that they will be *"crucified with Christ"* and dead to self, rejoicing in their salvation and enjoying the fruits of their redemption, and making personal holiness their primary concern;
- that they will expend their lives for the sheep and not expect the sheep to lay down their lives for their pastoral success;
- that they will not be hirelings, using the church and believers as stepping stones to advance personal ministry or acquire gain;
- that they will not be thieves who violate the integrity of the Body by ministering with malice or falsehood in order to achieve their own agendas, or robbers who forcefully inflict their will and 'fleece' the sheep;
- that they will not become as wolves who prey on the body and thus turn into an enemy of the flock of God;
- that their sense of protectiveness will not be for their own safety or reputation but for the sheep and their unity;

- that they will know their sheep, for where there is no personal knowledge there is little motivation to love redemptively and sacrificially;
- that they will faithfully proclaim, not a morality, but a redemption, a gospel of costly blood, not cheap grace;
- that their understanding of what it means to be a 'good' pastor will not be influenced or limited by managerial tasks that define a good performance, but by a deep and intimate knowledge of Christ their Redeemer, that not only transforms their lives daily but empowers them to communicate that goodness to others.

Jesus is the GREAT SHEPHERD: He will raise

"May the God of peace, who through the blood of the eternal covenant brought back from the dead our Lord Jesus, the great shepherd of the sheep, equip you with everything good for doing His will." (Hebrews 13: 20-21)

This magnificent finale of Hebrews is significantly prefaced by the writer's appeal: *"Pray for us ... I particularly urge you to pray ..."* (13:18-19) He applies his deep pastoral concern for his listeners to himself, humbly recognizing his need for their intercession for the worthy exercise of his spiritual responsibility. The focus here is the 'greatness' of Jesus' shepherding, demonstrated in his death for the sheep and supremely manifested in the resurrection, by which victory was secured over the devil, the great enemy of the flock, and by which we remain the recipients of the Lord's active post-resurrection shepherding through the power of the Holy Spirit. If our shepherd has overcome death, the ultimate enemy, then there is no enemy that he cannot protect us from. We can be assured forever of His compassionate care for us. Furthermore, such resurrection power convinces us that He can recover for us all that has been lost, and He can make available to us, all the resources that we need for life and godliness.

Ask God for pastors...

- that they will be daily filled with the resurrection power of the Holy Spirit;

- that peace will be a fruit of their reconciling ministry and that covenant faithfulness will characterize their relationships;

- that they will expect the gifts of the risen Christ to be generously dispensed to the church and evident and maturing in the flock they serve, and they will be skilled in encouraging and nurturing the manifestations of the Holy Spirit in the public services as well as in private;

- that they will be empowered and emboldened to raise up and equip (literally "put in proper condition") the saints, to prepare the church for works of service, thus encouraging and facilitating renewal in a manner that is both appropriate and resourceful;

- that they will not be threatened by the resurrection-giftedness of others, or tempted to make people and ministries their servants rather than the servants of Jesus and His church;

- that they will not be tempted to think that pastoral care is their sole responsibility and defined only by what they do, but that they will have a joyful understanding and infectious expectation of the shepherding presence of the resurrected Christ among the flock.

Jesus is the SHEPHERD OF SOULS: He will restore
"He himself bore our sins in his body on the tree so that we might die to sins and live for righteousness; by His wounds you have been healed. For you were like sheep going astray, but now you have returned to the Shepherd and Overseer of your souls." (1 Peter 2:24-25)

By referring to Isaiah 53, Peter is emphasizing the fact that Jesus' death for us is absolute proof of His identification with us, and His involvement in our lives. Yes, Jesus died for sin, but in doing so, He fulfilled the great purpose of it all, which was to bring us to God. Jesus was not only a suffering servant, but also a searching shepherd, committed to restore us to relationship with His Father. Furthermore, he was not only a searching shepherd but a securing one, for he is described as our 'overseer' who watches over those under His care. The one who guides us into God's fold is the same one who guards us once we have been secured there.

Ask God for pastors...

- that they will be identified with the sorrow of the lost and be involved restoratively in their recovery;
- that they will be used to minister healing to all who return, and gifted to raise up healing and prayer and discipleship ministry in the church;
- that pastoral ministry will have more to do with the restoration of souls than the reorganization of systems, with the renewal of spirits than the refurbishment of buildings;
- that ministry will be more committed to the protection of the sheep than the programmatic self-promotion of the fold;
- that the necessity to reach out and gather those who are astray will not be neglected because of the need to guard those who have been found;
- that they will be spiritually skilled in leading people to God's fold, not their church;
- that pastors and their spouses and families will know the restorative ministry of Jesus in their lives;
- that the 'mending' ministry will both supply what is

needed and restore what is broken;

- that the establishment of believers and the evangelization of unbelievers will never be separated, and that pastors will be equipped to both succor the saved and seek the lost;
- that alertness and watchfulness will characterize their oversight of the church.

Jesus is the CHIEF SHEPHERD: He will reward

"I appeal as a fellow elder, a witness of Christ's sufferings ... Be shepherds of God's flock ... not because you must, but because you are willing, as God wants you to be; not greedy for money, but eager to serve; not lording it over those entrusted to you, but being examples to the flock. And when the Chief Shepherd appears, you will receive the crown of glory that will never fade away." (1 Peter 5:1-4)

Again, note that the appeal to shepherd is based on Christ's sufferings. The value of the flock and of pastoral ministry can only be understood in terms of the blood-price that Christ paid for it. Pastors must never be tempted to see the church's value any other way. Peter presents both the call and the conduct of pastors, but he is more concerned here with why they minister than how they do so. The emphasis is on the hidden motivations of the heart, not the evident works of the hand. The Lord's appearing reminds us that there will be an accounting. This was why Spurgeon urged his pastoral candidates to "live as under the immediate eye of God and as in the blaze of the great all-revealing day." But like Peter, he reminded them that the Chief Shepherd would evaluate and reward them.

Ask God for pastors...

- that they will minister with an awareness that they will give an account of their stewardship, not ultimately to a Board, a denomination or a movement but to Jesus;

- that they will seek spiritual reward not material remuneration and guard against using the Lord's work as a means to financial gain;
- that they will covet the approval of God more than the applause of man;
- that they will continually realize that they are entrusted with sheep because of the cross, not entitled to them because of their charisma;
- that they will be saved from the temptations to human power and retain their integrity by freely submitting to the Lord, to fellow elders and to the flock, thus acknowledging accountability to God and man, while humbly seeking the wisdom of many godly counselors;
- that they will be an example to the flock, which implies that they are known by their lives as they relate to people "up close", not merely by their words as they speak from a podium "up there";
- that they will be encouraged and motivated by the fact that their labors are not in vain, that the Lord sees what no one else does, so that when unappreciated by the sheep, they will know the appreciation of the Chief Shepherd.

5 Asking That Pastors Be (Part 2)

"If anyone sets his heart on being an overseer,
he desires a noble task."
— 1 Timothy 3:1

Several scriptural sources inform us of some of the qualifications for pastoral ministry, demands which are high in standard, broad in scope and deep in specificity. One writer, Alexander Strauch, describes it like this: *"Proper qualification is a scriptural imperative, objective requirement, moral obligation, indispensable standard, and absolute necessity for those who would serve as leaders in the church."* Passages such as 1 Timothy 3:1-7, Titus 1:6-9, and 1 Peter 5:1-4, specifically indicate those requirements and responsibilities that need to be met and maintained by those who serve the Lord and His Body. These passages teach us the qualities of character and standards of conduct that we ask of God for pastors. The spiritual fitness of a church is inseparably linked to the spiritual fitness of the pastoral leaders. Read and meditate on each passage, make your own ask-notes and add other scriptural references that come to mind.

There are four major areas to ask about according to scripture:

Personal life and character

Ask for pastors to be: blameless, temperate, self-controlled, sober, gentle, not quarrelsome, not a lover of money, not overbearing or quick-tempered, a lover of what is good, upright, holy and disciplined, willing and eager to serve.

Order in relationships and in the home

Ask for pastors to be: faithful and loving in their marriage, a good parent and manager of his own family, seeing that their children obey them with proper respect (for if a pastor does not know how to manage their own family, how can they take care of God's family.)

Knowledge of God's Word

Ask God for pastors to be: firmly grounded in their understanding of the gospel, able to encourage and exhort others by sound doctrine and to refute those who oppose it; able to teach, to expound scripture (not just teach topics) and impart knowledge sufficiently for distortions of the truth to be discerned and rejected.

Reputation in the church and the community

Ask God for pastors to be: free from the pursuit of dishonest gain, known as an example to the flock, hospitable, not a recent convert, well-respected by outsiders in the neighborhood, as well as by those in the church community, as one with a good reputation.

Ask for all these areas of qualification to be satisfied in those becoming pastors, and increasingly mature and evident in the lives of those presently serving as pastors.

6 Ask God That Pastors Do (Part 1)

P*rivately*

Eugene Petersen, in his book *Working the Angles,* observes that the acts of praying, reading scripture and giving spiritual direction, determine the shape of pastoral ministry. However, because these acts are largely private and do not call attention to themselves, they are often not attended to. He writes that he knows of no 'profession' in which it is quite as easy to fake it. *"We can impersonate a pastor without being a pastor. The problem though, is that while we can get by with it in our communities, often with applause, we can't get by with it by ourselves. Some of us get restive. The restiveness does not come from Puritan guilt: we are doing what we are paid to do. It comes from another dimension — a vocational memory, a spiritual hunger. Being the kind of pastor that satisfies a congregation is one of the easiest jobs on the face of the earth — if we are satisfied with satisfying congregations."* This is what Spurgeon called *"the temptation to ministerialism."* Pastors need to take care of the private interior angles of their lives.

Moses was a great Old Testament shepherd. Looking after really woolly sheep in the backside of a desert for forty years is not most people's idea of pastoral training. It does seem that he learned to commune with God there. Exodus 34 describes the fruits of his private communion and is an excellent ask-list for pastors. Check it out and pray it out. We learn here that **communication with people** should be the product of **communion with God.** Ask for these same fruits for pastors:

Worship: "Moses bowed... and worshiped." (v8)

Relationship: "I am making a covenant with you." (v10)

Revelation: "The Lord said, 'Write down these words ...'" (v27)

Personal change: "Moses' ... face was radiant." (v29)

Ministry: "Afterward the Israelites came near him and he gave them all the commands the Lord had given him." (v32)

Allow the Word and the Spirit to amplify each point as you ask God for these fruits for pastors. Note the sequence. The actual pastoral ministry was the last thing, the result of personal engagement and process with God. All the elements of private devotion are here: giving attention to God, receiving His attention, and showing attentiveness to others. Ask God for these outcomes.

Publicly

Let us take another Old Testament passage. "Behold, the Lord God will come with a strong hand, and His arm shall **rule** for Him; behold, His reward is with Him, and His work before Him. He shall **feed** His flock like a shepherd: He shall **gather** the lambs with His arm, and **carry** them in His bosom, and shall gently **lead** those that are with young." (Isaiah 40: 10-11) The five active verbs emphasized here read like a pastoral 'to do' list. They provide the one who is asking for pastors with direction when praying for the actions of pastoral ministry. Again, let us compile some ask-notes, affirming the necessity for each of these acts to be present in pastoral work.

- **Rule** — Ask God that the basis of strength for pastoral leadership will not be personality or organizational qualifications but a son's or daughter's heart that expresses the loving authority of the Father and His Son Jesus, through hands that influence by personal touch. Ask for both the *"laying on of hands"* (representing the dispensing of spiritual blessing) and the *"shaking of hands"* (representing personal involvement that encourages friendship, fellowship and family). When private agendas and personal pride infect pastoral ministry, then gentle rule becomes Gentile rule (Luke 22:25) as the imposition of human will displaces the peaceable will of Christ. Ask God that pastors will be protected from the snares of human power, both in their hearts, as well as in the hearts of men and women around them. Ask that they will be saved from insecurity and the temptation to seek assurance in their position. Ask that they will be executors of the living Christ's will and not executives of a dead work. Ask that their 'rule' will be characterized by spiritual ministration, not secular management.

- **Feed** — There can be no leading without feeding. Ask God that pastors commit themselves to the study of God's Word so that the church receives a diet of 'meat' not 'skimmed milk.' You cannot grow a community of faith on a 'thought for the day.' Ask that congregations will be sensitive to pastors' needs for quality time for preparation, and that they will pray for their pastoral engagement with the Word. A nineteenth century Presbyterian New York pastor, Gardiner Spring, was passionate about the need to ask God for your pastor, especially for his call to feed the flock. He wrote: *"If a people are looking for rich sermons from their minister, their prayers must supply him with the needed material. If they seek for faithful sermons, their prayers must urge him by a full and uncompromising manifestation of the truth to commend himself to every man's conscience in the sight of God. If God's people are going to expect powerful and successful sermons, their prayers must make him a blessing to the souls of men. Would they have him come to them in the* *fullness of the blessings of the gospel of peace with a pounding heart and a burning eye and a glowing tongue and with sermons bathed in tears and filled with prayer? If so, their prayers must urge him to pray and their tears inspire his thrilling heart with the strong yearnings of Christian affection. It is in their own closets that the people of God most effectively challenge their beloved ministers to take heed to the ministry they have received from the Lord Jesus."* Faithful exposition of scripture by the pastor will produce a fervent expectation of God among the people. Authority in leadership will degenerate into human authoritarianism when it neglects to expound the authoritative Word of God and when it fails to submit to that Word's rule of truth. Without such feeding there is no church growth, regardless of the numbers. True, certain well-documented factors make for rapid expansion, but unless the mulch of Christ's truth is laid at the root, there will be no long-term fruit, even though the foliage may look impressive. Ask God for pastors who will not be tempted to spray leaves when they should be feeding roots. Ask that they will not devote their energies to the community's physical appearance when they should be minding its diet.

- **Gather** — Intrinsic to the pastoral gifting is a spiritual capacity to be a gatherer of sheep to the fold, and then a keeper of sheep in the fold. Not everyone who preaches can gather. Not everyone who stands behind a pulpit is a pastor. *Ekklesia*, the common word for church, is simply a 'gathering'. Throughout scripture God presents Himself as a gatherer and He has so many purposes in doing so. As gatherers, pastors desire those divine purposes to be fulfilled in the gatherings they oversee: the expectation of the presence of the Lord that touches everyone in a way that imprints His fingerprints of grace and goodness, of encouragement and healing upon them; the anticipation of hearing Him speak, a little perhaps through speakers but a lot through all the brothers and sisters around them through whom His manifold wisdom flashes when we gather (according to Paul anyway); the experience of union and unity in relationship and fellowship as they are the gathering of God in Christ; the experience of joy as we enact another dress-rehearsal for the gathering that is to come; the celebration of Jesus, the Bishop of our souls, our pastor, our gatherer, who came to fulfill the gathering purposes of God. He was described as one who would gather wheat into His barn like a reaper, gather sheep into His fold like a shepherd, gather people to His love like a mother hen her chicks, and also gather nations, like the sovereign Lord of all the earth. Ask for this gathering-giftedness for pastors, gathering people to be in union with Jesus, not just in membership in a church. Ask that they will be empowered to keep what they have gathered, and personally and practically nurture the members and encourage their incorporation and integration into the family and the work of the Lord. No ministry is self-generating so ask that they will always gather for and to the Chief Shepherd, Jesus, and thus avoid the temptation to gather people to themselves or their reputation. Ask that they will gather in a manner that bonds people with Jesus rather than binds them to a wrong dependence on human leadership.

- **Carry** — Carrying is an important aspect of caring in pastoral ministry. Defenseless lambs were often picked up by the shepherds and tucked inside their thick outer coat. Sometimes sheep need to be carried. Ask for pastors to be sensitive but also realistic about people's needs, especially when they struggle to cope and need protection and strengthening. Ask that they will be saved from the kind of busyness that only gives time for a quick word on the phone when what is required may be a face to face. Such benevolent caring will model the way we are to bear one another's burdens. Ask for the emotional, spiritual, mental and physical fortitude and effectiveness of pastors as they take upon themselves the weight of such ministry, which of course, none of them can bear alone, but they can serve as a teacher and example to all in the community who are gifted to carry those who need carried.

- **Lead** — The fact is that sheep need a shepherd. For Israel, Moses asked the Lord to *"appoint a man over this community to go out and come in before them, one who will lead them out and bring them in, so the Lord's people will not be like sheep without a shepherd."* (Numbers 27:15-17) The Lord has provided for the spiritual oversight of the church. Ask God for shepherds who will give the sheep a sense of place (belonging somewhere secure) and a sense of pace (going somewhere safely). You cannot overdrive sheep, especially when they are with young, and there are times when leadership expresses itself in the way in which a shepherd checks the rear of the flock. This ensures that his lead is never divorced from their need. Ask for a pastoral leadership that considers the safety of the flock before their own preservation. Ask that pastors will truly know the flock they lead, so that they will not follow a stranger. Ask that at a time when pastors are bombarded with literature about leadership stratagems and practices and techniques, they will not neglect to also study the example of Jesus with increasing delight and expectation, and thus be saved from adopting models that though pragmatically effective, and culturally relevant, may end up being spiritually deficient. Sheep need shepherds, not wolves in sheepskin jackets.

7 Ask God That Pastors Do (Part 2)

What we are doing is taking some sample scriptural passages from both Old and New Testaments, with their instructions and examples, and encouraging each other to ask God for pastors, in a way that accords with His will and His word for them. Make it a practice to pray with an open Bible and pray the Word. For example, take Psalm 23, arguably one of the best-known passages in the Bible.

> "The Lord is my shepherd, I lack nothing. He makes me lie down in green pastures, He leads me beside quiet waters, He refreshes my soul. He guides me along the right paths for His name's sake. Even though I walk through the darkest valley, I will fear no evil, for you are with me; your rod and your staff, they comfort me. You prepare a table before me in the presence of my enemies. You anoint my head with oil; my cup overflows. Surely your goodness and love will follow me all the days of my life, and I will dwell in the house of the Lord forever."

Sadly, many people know the psalm but not the Shepherd it describes. These scriptures present the attributes and actions of a true shepherd, particularly the intimate involvement with the flock. This psalm deftly but indelibly presents the pastor-shepherd not only as one who gives the flock spiritual direction according to his knowledge of where they need to go, but also as one who is willing to have his route and his approach mapped by the immediate needs of the sheep. Consequently, Psalm 23 is an intriguing example for pastors, and a sure guide for those who ask God for them. Meditate upon it and develop your own specific prayer list.

- **The Lord is my shepherd:** Ask that pastors will submit themselves to the Lord's ministry and acknowledge His superiority as shepherd and their security as members of the flock. As a pastor I have always assumed that I am the neediest member in that flock.

- **I shall lack nothing:** Ask that they will preach and teach the fullness of God's provision and minister Christ's life and sufficiency with conviction and assurance.

- **He makes me lie down in green pastures:** Ask that they will have a sensitivity to the flock's need, especially the need to feed on the Word of God, but also to digest the truth and assimilate and practice its benefits; that they will show people how to rest in the Lord and wait on God and for God; that rest and not rush will mark their ministry; that churches will be filled with grazing sheep not stampeding cattle.

- **He leads me beside quiet waters:** Sheep are fearful of swiftly moving water, so ask that pastors will beware of human limitations and uncertainties yet be skilled to discern those strategic times and special touches that bring sustenance; that care will be intimate not intermittent; that pastoral ministry will be responsive to immediate human need; that it will lead people to spiritual refreshment, not drive them into an enforced, 'canned' and conformist spirituality.

- **He restores my soul:** The fact is that sheep wander, so ask that pastors will be used to minister restoration to the strays and the wounded, reassurance to the weak and hesitant, revival to the weary and listless; that the 'cure of souls' will mark pastoral ministry and none will be lost.

- **He guides me in paths of righteousness:** Ask that pastors will be examples of obedience and faithful to preach and teach all the demands of the gospel in a way that is not culturally selective, but scripturally comprehensive; that deals truly with sin but tenderly with the sinner.

- **For His name's sake:** Ask that pastors will not be tempted by any need to establish their personal name or the name of their church, but that everything they preach and practice will clearly draw attention to the surpassing need to honor Jesus' name and avoid anything that will shame it.

- **Even though I walk through the valley of the shadow of death I will fear no evil, for you are with me; your rod and your staff, they comfort me:** Ask that pastors will be enabled to be biblically realistic and yet triumphant in dealing with pain and suffering and that they will be equipped with the 'rod' and the 'staff', the symbols of defense and discipline, as they walk with people through circumstances in which both loving protection and firm guidance will have to be exercised; that the power of the resurrection will be the keynote of their ministry in the domain of disease and death.

- **You prepare a table before me in the presence of my enemies. You anoint my head with oil; my cup overflows. Surely goodness and mercy will follow me all the days of my life and I will dwell in the house of the Lord forever:** Ask that pastors will be able to minister the goodness of God with a master chef's skill in preparation, and a maître d'hotel's eye for detail, and with a waiter's commitment to serve; that despite the pressures and distractions of contending enemies they will not forget to dispense the oil of blessing and healing; that they will not cease to pour out their own lives that others may discover the goodness of God's grace and mercy; that the flock will know that God's provision is not contingent upon good times only but that His covenant goodness and fatherly love will follow them all the days of their life; that pastors will see their responsibility to care for the sheep to the very gate of heaven, from dedicating the child to conducting the funeral, when all shall dwell in the house of the Lord forever. That will be church!

8. Why Do Sheep Scatter?

Let me suggest another angle that will highlight the responsibilities of pastoral ministry and why pastors need to be prayed for. Why do sheep scatter? Have you ever asked that question? At the beginning of this booklet, when we checked our immigration and customs, we acknowledged that sometimes sheep scatter. Things happen that dislodge and scatter believers from their places of community. The reason I am suggesting that this is a good question for you to ask is because the biblical answers to it will help you know what to ask of God for pastors. Why? In addressing this question the Bible has little to say about sheep but a lot to say about the responsibility, accountability and culpability of shepherds. What follows is a contribution to fuel your own biblically-based asking. Some of the points will dovetail, reinforce and overlap some of the things already observed and asked for. It will help you to ask:

> **FOR:** certain pastoral qualities and characteristics;
> **AGAINST:** particular temptations and attacks.

Smitten
"Strike the shepherd, and the sheep will be scattered."
(Zechariah 13:7)

Jesus quoted this himself in Mark 14:27, and then we read, *"everyone deserted him and fled."* (Mark 14:50) When shepherds are smitten, whether by the sin that is within or the attacks that are without, sheep are in great danger. Ask God for the protection of pastors, that they take heed to their own spiritual security as they walk in the light and war against darkness. Addressing pastors in his timeless book *The Reformed Pastor* (1656), Richard Baxter wrote about the enemy's tactics to subvert the church: *"He knows what a rout he may make among the rest if the leaders fall before their eyes."* For this reason, we ask for protection for pastors: for their spiritual fullness and fervor; for their mental acuity and discernment; for their physical health; for their sexual purity; for their emotional peace and stability; for their marital fidelity and family unity. Pastoring is emotionally demanding, and vulnerable to many discouragements and disappointments that sometimes strike and smite deep in the heart. Spurgeon warned pastors about those offensives of the enemy against them that are often *"attacks in the direction of depression."* It also ought to be said that sometimes sheep scatter precisely because the shepherd does take a stand on a matter of truth, and take a blow, which turns out to be uncomfortable, or culturally embarrassing for many, and it is the truth, not the enemy of truth, that scatters them. The main way that the enemy seeks to destroy the flock is by attacking the shepherd. In asking for the safety of shepherds you are praying against the enemy getting a foothold in the fold. Consider and pray through the many ways and means that the enemy uses to smite pastors (pressures, divisions, heresies, discouragements, temptations, family matters, accusations, disloyalties, physical issues, provision). Ask specifically about these and other matters in relation to the protection of your pastor.

Sleeping
"Your shepherds slumber… your people are scattered."
(Nahum 3:18)

Though addressed to the King of Assyria, the image shows that a dereliction of duty spells danger for the flock. Ask that pastors will be characterized by watchfulness as they exercise their guardianship: *"Keep watch over yourselves and all the flock of which the Holy Spirit has made you overseers."* (Acts 20:28) In Mark

13:33, Jesus says to his disciples, *"Be on guard. Be alert!"* The literal idea being conveyed here by his use of words is "chasing sleep". There are so many demands and desires that can lure the servants of God into distractions and lull them into day-dreams (though these are often dressed up as great visions). On top of all this, if you have not got the idea by now, there is the pressure of sheer weariness that accompanies legitimate spiritual labor. But there is also the spiritual slumber that comes from laziness and withdrawal from action. There was a poem that I had to study at school called *The Lotos-Eaters* by Lord Tennyson:

> *Surely, surely, slumber is more sweet than toil, the shore*
> *Than labor in the deep mid-ocean, wind and wave and oar.*

Part of Spurgeon's legacy is his 'Lectures to my Students', a rich source for knowledge about how to pray for pastors. He wrote: *"The solemn work with which the Christian ministry concerns itself demands a man's all, and that all at its best. To engage in it half-heartedly is an insult to God and man. Slumber must forsake our eyelids sooner than men shall be allowed to perish."* Study all the injunctions in the New Testament that tell us what to consider, meditate upon, take heed to, continue in, persevere in, guard and perceive. Such commands usually demand an intensive application of the mind to the things of God — an earnest contemplation, a vigorous apprehension. Ask for these capacities of heart and mind for pastors, for the renewal of their minds, for the mind of Christ, for concentration and awakedness. Ask that the sleep that scripture says leads to impoverishment will be chased away. Ask for an unprecedented revivedness among pastors.

Senseless

"They are shepherds who lack understanding; they all turn to their own way, each seeks his own gain ... The shepherds are senseless and do not inquire of the Lord; so they do not prosper and all their flock is scattered." (Isaiah 56:11; Jeremiah 10:21)

Senselessness is essentially the abandonment of God's way of doing things and the adoption of an agenda scripted more by personal perceptions, predispositions and preferences. A conversation with self and others replaces prayer. The root problem here is specific: the failure to *"inquire of the Lord."* We are asking that pastors will be asking of God! (No wonder that Spurgeon made the matter of private and public prayer the core content of pastoral training.) When introspection replaces intercession the result is spiritual insanity. Of course, when one is talking to oneself, one never asks a question that one cannot answer. It is a small pool of knowledge and understanding that leads quickly to spiritually senseless decisions. The ultimate senselessness is when shepherds become successful in their leadership, and become beguiled by flattery and pride, and people end up being led into a wasteland of error and spiritual oblivion. *"My people have been lost sheep; their shepherds have led them astray and caused them to roam in the mountains. They wandered over mountain and hill and forgot their own resting place."* (Jeremiah 50:6) Ask that pastors inquire of the Lord, recovering God's thoughts and discovering His will as they too ask of God with an open Word. Ignorance and senselessness are presented as violent enemies that scatter the flock. Ask for a pastorate that is instructed in the Word and informed of the devil's devices (Ephesians 6:10-18) and therefore knows what to ask for the flock, as they stay in touch with God, with the people and with what is going on in the world. Paul's pastoral training of Timothy was clear: *"Take heed to yourself and to the doctrine."* (1 Timothy 3:16) To avoid senselessness, ask that they will experience in fullness *"the Spirit who is from God, that we may understand what God has freely given us."* (1 Corinthians 2:12) Clearly, whenever there is a lack of godly understanding, then personal intuition and insight will replace the instruction of scripture. The wisdom of God will be contaminated by the wisdom of this world, and cultural truisms will replace divine truth. More is needed than drive-through sermons and a spiritual snack culture, what used to be called "sermonettes for Christianettes." It makes **sense** to ask that pastors be filled with the Spirit and filled with the Word

(Ephesians 5:18; Colossians 3:16), not only to deliver the truth but to landscape it to the different shapes and contours of people's lives and circumstances.

Selfish

"Woe to the shepherds of Israel who only take care of themselves! Should not shepherds take care of the flock?... So they were scattered ..." (Ezekiel 34:2-5)

Selfishness is the inevitable consequence of senselessness and moral stupidity. When shepherds are consumed with their own concerns, Ezekiel says that the sheep are not only scattered but slaughtered, because of the consequences of pastoral neglect that leads to a failure to: strengthen the weak, heal the sick, bind up the injured, call back the strays and seek the lost (v4). Preaching on this scripture, St. Augustine condemned those pastors who preached and promised worldly gain and prosperity to justify their own lusts and ambitions. Has as much been smuggled into the atonement as current heretical teaching has done? *"But what sort of shepherds are they who not only fail to prepare the sheep for temptations, but even promise them worldly happiness. God himself made no such promise ... But you shepherd, who seek what is yours and not what is Christ's, you disregard what the apostle says!"* The sheep are scattered by shepherds who use them for their own gain. *"Praise the Lord I am rich! Their own shepherds do not spare them."* (Zechariah 11:5) The prophet goes on to describe the effects of this selfishness as *"tearing off their hoofs."* In other words, the sheep have no mobility. Life is going nowhere. The prophet says that if the shepherd is consumed with self, the sheep will be consumed by wild animals, a graphic image for false teaching and false shepherding. Selfishness is sometimes manifested in self-preservation, as we see in the example of the hireling that Jesus gives in John 10:12, who runs to save his own skin and thus abandons the sheep. *"Then the wolf attacks the flock and scatters it."* You heard it from the Chief Shepherd. Ask that pastors will not be tempted by the deceitfulness of riches, by a love for the world and the things that are in the world. Ask that God will expose those who defraud God's kingdom by turning the public sanctuary into a private business, by trading on people's trust, and counterfeiting the power of God with charlatan trickery and bombastic rhetoric. Ask that the church will wisely and justly provide for pastors, in a manner that fulfills the scriptural obligations to take care of the teaching elders. When someone is taken up with their deserts in ministry, they are one step from becoming a deserter from their calling, and one step from causing sheep to disperse and scatter. Ask that Paul's statement will be truly the desire of all pastors: *"I will not be a burden to you, because what I want is not your possessions but you."* (2 Corinthians 12:14) God's word to the selfish shepherds is blunt: *"I am against the shepherds and will hold them accountable for my flock. I will remove them from tending the flock so that the shepherds can no longer feed themselves."* (Ezekiel 34:10) Also note that selfishness results in division and contention among the sheep, which also leads to scattering. (Ezekiel 34:20-21)

Sloppy
"Woe to the shepherds who are destroying and scattering the sheep of my pasture ... you have scattered my flock and driven them away and have not bestowed care on them." (Jeremiah 23:1-2)

Negligence will scatter a flock. Jeremiah has a severe word to say about it: *"A curse on him who is lax in doing the Lord's work."* (Jeremiah 48:10) Ask that pastors will have a zeal that is directed by love and a knowledge that is dynamited by godly enthusiasm. Ask that those scriptures that encourage diligence will be their guide and that they will guard the rigors of their own discipleship. Baxter warned pastors of the enemy's work against them in this matter: *"Oh what a conquest will he think he hath if he can make a minister lazy and unfaithful."* (The Reformed Pastor) Ask that they will be saved from delegating to others that which they have been called to discharge and that they will not take short-cuts in their preparation of the Word to be taught to the people. *"Be sure that you know the condition of your flocks; give careful attention to your herds."* (Proverbs 27:23) Ask that they will be appropriately methodical and thorough in their service.

Strangers
"They will never follow a stranger; in fact, they will run away from him because they do not recognize a stranger's voice." (John 10:5)

To confer the title 'Pastor' does not of itself bequeath pastoral ministry. Jesus himself taught that not all who work in the fold are necessarily shepherds. There is a big difference between the one who truly looks **after** sheep and the one who just looks **at** them. Jesus said that the basic mark of a stranger is that he *"cares nothing for the sheep."* Read John 10 again and use it to ask for pastors, that they will carry the crook as Jesus did. Ask that the voice of Jesus will clearly be heard through them, rather than the teachings and emphases that are so often attached to the name of a man or a movement. The divine voice is the antidote to scattering, because Jesus said His sheep *"follow Him because they know His voice ... I know my sheep and my sheep know me ... they too will listen to my voice."* (John 10: 4, 14-15) Ask that pastors will be known, not as strangers, but as friends of Jesus and therefore, like Jesus, friends of saints and sinners.

Scarce
"The people wander like sheep oppressed for lack of a shepherd." (Zechariah 10:2)

Last, but not least, here is an important reason why some sheep remain scattered and oppressed. Their need for a shepherd is not met. Every spiritual generation needs shepherds after God's heart. In some nations, pastors are scarce simply because they are persecuted and imprisoned. We should ask that for every one incarcerated by the authorities, many more will be raised up in their place so that the sheep will be tended and taught and secured against scattering. In the West, we should be asking for more pastors, not just for bigger churches; for an army of pastors that are going to take care of the millions that are going to turn to Christ in answer to our prayers. Ask that your church will become an incubator for the pastoral ministry and that the examples of those who are pastors will persuade a new generation that it is a high calling to nurture the saints and lay down one's life at the door of the fold. Ask for those around the world who are presently called and in training. Gather information on what God is doing in church-planting in your nation, or in Bible Schools and Theological Colleges that honor Christ and His Word. Encourage your church to invest a significant amount of its mission endeavor and resource to raising up pastors in the nations. Ask for a move of the Holy Spirit in the seminaries, and for a preparation that equips for what will be encountered in the ministry. Ask that those presently pastoring will be given discernment to recognize the pastoral gifts and callings of God in those they care for. Like David, many future shepherds are not "out there somewhere" but already in the sheepfold. Let there be no scarcity of shepherds, so that there will be no needless oppression upon God's people.

Perhaps you know someone who is "scattered". I think we all do. It is said that in any major city there are tens of thousands of scattered believers, many of them in a back-slidden state, disconnected and drifting further away as time passes. Ask God for an unprecedented gathering of the strays who have scattered for whatever reason, and for pastors and churches who will be ready to welcome and receive them.

9 THE APPEAL: ASK FOR PASTORS... ASK FOR US

I am now appealing to you as a pastor on behalf of pastors. Ask of God for us! It is clear, is it not, just from these few pages of scriptures that help us how to ask for pastors, that it is an awesome calling that requires a wide range of tasks and carries huge responsibilities and accountabilities. How can we not ask for pastors? How foolish is it not to? How impossible is the task without such asking for them? Such appeals, "Ask for us", have come from generations of pastors. This is not an original cry, but it has to be raised in every generation. There is an inviolable relationship between an asking pastor and an asking congregation, between a preaching pastor and a praying people. Do you remember the passionate plea of James Smith in the introduction? Listen to him again: *"The ministers of Christ NEED the prayers of their people, their work is arduous, their weakness is great, their foes are furious, and their hindrances are many. They DESIRE the prayers of their people, for they know that prayer has power with God, and brings down great and invaluable blessings. The prayers of the people influence the preaching of the minister, and no people should ever expect their minister to preach successfully, or to their souls' profit, except they are much in prayer for him. As the prayers of the people influence the preaching of the minister, so the preaching of the minister influences the prayers of the people. The people therefore ought so to pray as to bring down gifts and grace on the minister; and the minister ought so to preach as to stir up the minds of the people, to seek these great blessings from the Lord. We are mutually dependent the one on the other. **Ministers cannot get on well, except prayer is made without ceasing by the church to God for them;** neither can the church prosper, except the minister preaches the gospel* *with savor, unction, and the Holy Spirit sent down from Heaven."*

Commentators have often observed that Paul was the only apostle who specifically, again and again, asked his readers to ask for him. Adolph Saphir, a nineteenth century Presbyterian pastor, a Hungarian Messianic Jew, wrote one of the most influential books on prayer, *The Hidden Life,* and observed this about Paul: *"He who labored more than the other apostles, and who was endowed with so many gifts, seems to have had the greatest craving for sympathy, for affection, for communion, and the most vivid conception that God only giveth the increase; that it is not by might nor by power, but by the Spirit of the Lord."* Arthur Pink, another well-known commentator, writes: *"If, then, the greatest of the apostles stood in need of the intercessory support of his brethren, how much more so the rank and the file of God's ministers."* In the mouth of three witnesses a thing is confirmed: *"If Paul with all his gifts, graces, and success, thus prized and requested the prayers of the Lord's people for himself, then how much more may we; and with how much greater earnestness and importunity would we cry, Brethren, pray, pray, pray, for us!"* (James Smith) Paul is not just closing his letters in a polite manner and suggesting that they 'say a little prayer' for him if he crosses their minds. It is so important to catch the urgency in the request. In no less than seven of his epistles, Paul appeals for people to ask God for him. In the first of these below, he uses the word *sunagonizomai*, literally meaning *"agonize with"*. It is the same word Jesus uses before Pilate when He talks of a *"fight"*. (John 18:6) Paul the pastor is not asking for people to spare him a little prayerful thought, but to strive together with him at the place of asking God for specific things and specific outcomes in the battle.

"Now I beseech you, brethren, for the Lord Jesus Christ's sake, and for the love of the Spirit, that you strive together with me in your prayers to God for me." (Romans 15:30). *"... as you help us by your prayers ... Then many will give thanks on our behalf for the gracious favor granted us in answer to the prayers of many."* (2 Corinthians

1:11) *"Pray also for me, that whenever I open my mouth, words may be given me so that I will fearlessly make known the mystery of the gospel, for which I am an ambassador in chains. Pray that I may declare it fearlessly, as I should."* (Ephesians 6:19-20) *"And pray for us, too, that God may open a door for our message, so that we may proclaim the mystery of Christ, for which I am in chains. Pray that I may proclaim it clearly, as I should."* (Colossians 4:3-4) *"Brethren, pray for us."* (1 Thessalonians 5:25.) *"Finally, brethren, pray for us, that the Word of the Lord may have free course and be glorified, even as it is with you."* (2 Thessalonians 3:1) *"Pray for us. We are sure that we have a clear conscience and desire to live honorably in every way."* (Hebrews 13:18)

This entire booklet could have been an ask-list for pastors, just based on these pleas of Paul for the churches to ask God for him. For what? Go to these passages, in context, and you will find that the list would include asking for: safety and deliverance from physical attack, wisdom and understanding, direction, opportunity, unction to preach, boldness and power, spiritual strength, personal refreshment, a good conscience, spiritual protection, humility, stability, relationships, self-discipline, joy and on and on. Is anyone short of things to ask for? Do we still need to establish the ground for this appeal? Perhaps Pastor James Smith seems to think so.

"The past is gone, and gone forever. We may regret, we may deplore, we may wish it had been different but we cannot alter it now. Shall the present, the future, if any future is granted unto us be spent differently? Will you pray for your pastors more frequently, more sincerely, more urgently? Will you lay their case before the Lord, with more minuteness, more in detail, plead for them the promises of God's grace, and ask for them greater blessings, with greater fervor, in the precious name of Jesus? Will you? Will you? Can you justify your past conduct on this point? Are you satisfied with it? Have you not lost many, many a blessing, by neglecting to pray for your pastors; or by merely praying for them in a cold, customary, formal manner? Brethren,

we need your prayers! We beg your prayers. We beseech you to pray for us!"

So will you?

10 The Altar Call: Who Will Ask?

I am going to let Pastor James Smith, who just joined me in the appeal, also join me in the altar call. *"Believing as you do, that the success of the gospel depends on the blessing of God, and that the blessing of God is promised to the prayers of the saints: do you pray as much as you ought for the ministers of Christ? Again, think of the importance of the ministry to the Church. It is by the ministry: that the Lord's people are to be fed, instructed, and edified; that the weak are to be strengthened, the unruly warned, and the sorrowful comforted; that backsliders are to be restored, and wanderers be brought back to the fold. It is by the ministry, that error is to be refuted, and the truth of God preserved in its purity among us; that the Lord works in conversion, consolation, and restoration. If, therefore, the Church is to be increased, if believers are to be built up on their holy faith, if the sheep of Christ are to be folded and fed, it is of the greatest importance that our pastors be holy, energetic, and successful. But we have no right to expect to have the right people, or that they be preserved in the right spirit, or that they should be blessed and honored in their work, but in answer to the fervent effectual prayers of the Lord's people. Once more then, I ask, considering the importance of the ministry to the Church: do you pray as you ought, or as often as you should, for the stewards of the mysteries of God?"*

So whether it is Paul's voice, or the voices that I have quoted, whether it is my voice or your pastor's voice, we are all appealing together: "Ask God for us!" What is your response? You are probably reading this sitting down. If you have been exercised to ask God for your pastor in particular, and for the pastoral ministry in the church in general, and intend to do something about this, I am going to follow the pastoral appeal with an altar call and ask you to do something. Just get out of your chair right now, or from whatever position you are in, and stand before the Lord. Let's do two things.

A confession

Now, first of all, ask the Lord, whether silently, or out loud, for what you need. Confess it. Apply what you have just read by doing it immediately.

- Is there any need to ask for repentance? For prayerlessness perhaps? Is there any need to ask for healing for any unresolved attitude or pain that relates to any relationship with any church or pastor, that has possibly dulled the affections that pray? Is there any forgiveness that needs to be asked for as well as given?

- Is there any need for a renewed love for your pastor, for pastors, for the church? Ask the Lord to give you a fresh love for these. Some people talk and feel about the church as if she was a familiar old wife. No, she is always what Jesus calls His bride. We need to ask for pastors and people "as Christ loved the church." (Ephesians 5:25)

A commitment

Commit yourself to pray the Word for your pastor, for the pastors of your community and nation.

- Offer yourself as one who will ask for pastors, and ask for the interceding Holy Spirit to ask through you, giving you revelation as you ask according to the scriptures.

- Commit to study the scriptures yourself to give you more insight as to how to ask for pastors.

- If Jesus is not just the Good Shepherd but the very best shepherd, and if pastors are to walk in his footsteps because He has set them an example (1 Peter 3:21), then it follows that one of the very best ask-lists that you could assemble would be one that is developed from a fresh close study of Jesus in the Gospels. Take time to re-read and pray your way through them, making notes about the attributes and actions of Jesus that should characterize Christ-like pastoral ministry and begin to ask for these for your pastor and all pastors. Pay special attention to chapters like John 10 and 17.

- Study the lives of great pastor-shepherds in scripture like Moses or David, Paul or Peter.

- Do a word study on 'shepherd' and make your notes on how the image is used in context, especially in the psalms, the prophets and the epistles to express God's concern for His people and His pastors. Record specific scriptures that give you fuel for intercession for pastors.

- Study the "pastoral epistles" (1 and 2 Timothy, Titus and Philemon) so named because they contain the heart of Paul's instruction about pastoral work in the churches. These texts are a rich vein of counsel for a pastor's personal life and public ministry, for practical church concerns and for weightier doctrinal matters affecting church polity. List the specific instructions, images, encouragements, and warnings that Paul records, and apply them in your asking for your pastor and church.

- There are so many manifestations of the devil's enmity against the church. An instructive exercise for asking for pastors, is to go through all the epistles and make a note of the variety of problems, concerns, questions (relational, doctrinal, moral, societal) that each one addresses that are afflicting the life of the churches being addressed. This will serve as a salutary reminder of the range of assaults that pastors have to deal with on a regular basis, and will encourage you to ask for specific discernment for them in these areas, as well as Holy Spirit empowered skills to handle them.

- Perhaps you could send a note to your pastor or pastoral elders and let them know the Lord has given you a burden and that you will be asking on their behalf. Perhaps you could give them all a copy of this booklet to encourage them to ask for themselves, or maybe get a few copies for friends and form an 'ask-group' in your church community for the pastors, or maybe one in your town or city, to meet regularly and ask for the pastors of the area. If you do, we would love to know about it and get it on our ask-list. Go to www.asknetwork.net, and contact the relevant national site. Feel free to download any of the available resources for your ask-group.

11 Closing Prayers

The following three prayers are for pastors, but each of them is written by a pastor praying for himself. As you listen in, this will give you some further insight into what to ask for, and you can take their ask-points for themselves, and make them your own for asking for your pastors.

First prayer

O God, I know that I often do Your work without your power, and sin by my dead, heartless, blind service; my lack of inward light, love, delight; my mind, heart, tongue moving without Your help. I see my sinful heart in seeking the praise of others. This is my vileness — to seek my own glory. It is my deceit to preach and pray — in order to generate admiration; whereas I should consider myself more vile than any man in my own eyes. Help me to rejoice in my infirmities and to acknowledge my deficiencies before others. Keep me from high thoughts of myself or my work, for I am nothing but sin and weakness. In me no good dwells, and my best works are tainted with sin. Humble me to the dust before You. Root and tear out the poisonous weed of pride, and show me my utter nothingness. Keep me sensible of my sinnership. Sink me deeper into penitence. Break the 'Dagon' of pride in pieces before the ark of Your presence! Demolish the 'Babel' of self-importance and scatter it to the wind! Level to the ground my 'Jericho walls' of a haughty, rebel heart! Then grace, free grace, will be my experience and message. This is my ministry, my life, my prayer, my end. Grant me grace that I shall not fail. Amen.

(The prayer of a seventeenth century pastor)

Second prayer

O My Lord, Let not my ministry be approved only by men, or merely win the esteem and affections of people; but do the work of grace in their hearts, call in thy elect, seal and edify the regenerate ones, and command eternal blessing on their souls. Save me from self-opinion and self-seeking. Water the hearts of those who hear thy Word, that seed sown in weakness may be raised in power. Cause me and those that hear me to behold thee here in the light of special faith and hereafter in the blaze of endless glory. Make my every sermon a means of grace to myself, and help me to experience the power of thy dying love, for thy blood is balm, thy presence bliss, thy smile heaven, thy cross the place where truth and mercy meet. Look upon the doubts and discouragements of my ministry and keep me from self-importance. I beg pardon for my many sins, omissions, infirmities, as a man, as a minister. Command thy blessing on my weak, unworthy labors and on the message of salvation given. Stay with thy people and may thy presence be their portion and mine. When I preach to others let not my words be merely elegant and masterly, my reasoning polished and refined, my performance powerless and tasteless, but may I exalt thee and humble sinners. O Lord of power and grace, all hearts are in thy hands, all events at thy disposal. Set the seal of thy almighty will upon my ministry. Amen.

(Taken from 'The Valley of Vision: A Collection of Puritan Prayers,' edited by Arthur Bennett)

Third prayer

O Lord, I have heard Thy voice and was afraid. Thou hast called me to an awesome task in a grave and perilous hour. Thou art about to shake all nations and the earth and also heaven, that the things that cannot be shaken may remain. O Lord, our Lord, Thou has stopped to honor me to be Thy servant. No man takes this honor upon himself save he that is called of God, as was Aaron. Thou hast ordained me Thy messenger to them that are stubborn of heart and hard of hearing. They have rejected Thee, the Master, and it is not to be expected that they will receive me, the servant.

My God, I shall not waste time deploring my weakness nor my unfittedness for the work. The responsibility is not mine but Thine. Thou hast said, "I knew thee—I ordained thee—I sanctified thee," and Thou hast also said, "Thou shalt go to all that I shall send thee, and whatsoever I command thee thou shalt speak." Who am I to argue with Thee or to call into question Thy sovereign choice? The decision is not mine but Thine. So be it, Lord. Thy will, not mine, be done. Well do I know, Thou God of the prophets and the apostles, that as long as I honor Thee Thou wilt honor me. Help me therefore to take this solemn vow to honor Thee in all my future life and labors, whether by gain or by loss, by life or by death, and then to keep that vow unbroken while I live.

It is time, O God, for Thee to work, for the enemy has entered into Thy pastures and the sheep are torn and scattered. And false shepherds abound who deny the danger and laugh at the perils which surround Thy flock. The sheep are deceived by these hirelings and follow them with touching loyalty while the wolf closes in to kill and destroy. I beseech Thee, give me sharp eyes to detect the presence of the enemy; give me understanding to distinguish the false friend from the true. Give me vision to see and courage to report what I see faithfully. Make my voice so like Thine own that even the sick sheep will recognize it and follow Thee.

Lord Jesus, I come to Thee for spiritual preparation. Lay Thy hand upon me. Anoint me with the oil of the New Testament prophet. Forbid that I should become a religious scribe and thus lose my prophetic calling. Save me from the curse that lies dark across the face of the modern clergy, the curse of compromise, of imitation, of professionalism. Save me from the error of judging a church by its size, its popularity or the amount of its yearly offering. Help me to remember that I am a prophet; not a promoter, not a religious manager— but a prophet. Let me never become a slave to crowds. Heal my soul of carnal ambitions and deliver me from the itch for publicity. Save me from the bondage to things. Let me not waste my days puttering around the house. Lay Thy terror upon me, O God, and drive me to the place of prayer where I may wrestle with principalities and powers and the rulers of the darkness of this world. Deliver me from overeating and late sleeping. Teach me self-discipline that I may be a good soldier of Jesus Christ. I accept hard work and small rewards in this life. I ask for no easy place. I shall try to be blind to the little ways that I could make my life easier. If others seek the smoother path I shall try to take the hard way without judging them too harshly. I shall expect opposition and try to take it quietly when it comes. Or if, as sometimes it falleth out to Thy servants, I shall have grateful gifts pressed upon me by Thy kindly people, stand by me then and save me from the blight that often follows. Teach me to use whatever I receive in such manner that it will not injure my soul nor diminish my spiritual power. And if in Thy permissive providence honor should come to me from Thy church, let me not forget in that hour that I am unworthy of the least of Thy mercies, and that if men knew me as intimately as I know myself they would withhold their honors or bestow them upon others more worthy to receive them.

And now, O Lord of heaven and earth, I consecrate my remaining days to Thee; let them be many or few, as Thou wilt. Let me stand before the great or minister to the poor and lowly; that choice is not mine, and I would not influence it if I could. I am Thy servant to do Thy will, and that will is sweeter to me than position or riches or fame and I choose it above all things on earth or in heaven. Though I am chosen of Thee and honored by a high and holy calling, let me never forget that I am but a man of dust and ashes, a man with all the natural faults and passions that plague the race of men. I pray Thee therefore, my Lord and Redeemer, save me from myself and from all the injuries I may do myself while trying to be a blessing to others. Fill me with thy power by the Holy Spirit, and I will go in Thy strength and tell of Thy righteousness, even Thine only. I will spread abroad the message of redeeming love while my normal powers endure. Then, dear Lord, when I am old and weary and too tired to go on, have a place ready for me above, and make me to be numbered with Thy saints in glory everlasting. Amen.

(The prayer of a minor prophet. A.W.Tozer, 1950)

Appendix

Here is another resource to identify specific things to ask for your pastor/s.

Christ, The Example Of Ministers
by Jonathan Edwards

It is not only our great duty, but will be our greatest honor, to imitate Christ, and do the work that he has done, and so act as co-workers with him.

- The ministers of Christ should be persons of the same spirit that their Lord was of — the same spirit of humility and lowliness of heart; for the servant is not greater than his Lord.

- They should be of the same spirit of heavenly mindedness, and contempt of the glory, wealth, and pleasures of this world.

- They should be of the same spirit of devotion and fervent love to God. They should follow the example of his prayerfulness; of whom we read from time to time of his retiring from the world, away from the noise and applause of the multitudes, into mountains and solitary places, for secret prayer, and holy converse with his Father.

- Ministers should be persons:
    - of the same quiet, lamb-like spirit that Christ was of, the same spirit of submission to God's will, and patience under afflictions, and meekness towards men;

- of the same calmness and composure of spirit under reproaches and sufferings from the malignity of evil men;
- of the same spirit of forgiveness of injuries; of the same spirit of charity, of fervent love and extensive benevolence;
- of the same disposition to pity the miserable, to weep with those that weep, to help men under their calamities of both soul and body, to hear and grant the requests of the needy, and relieve afflicted;
- of the same spirit of condescension to the poor and lowly, tenderness and gentleness toward the weak, and great and effectual love to enemies.

- They should also be of the same spirit of zeal, diligence, and self-denial for the glory of God, and advancement for his kingdom, and for the good of mankind; for which things sake Christ went though the greatest labors, and endured the most extreme sufferings.

And in order to our imitating Christ in the work of the ministry, in any tolerable degree, we should not have our hearts weighed down, and time filled up with worldly affections, cares, and pursuits. The duties of a minister that have been recommended, are absolutely inconsistent with a mind much taken up with worldly profit, glory, amusements, and entertainments.